Liner Notes

Liner Notes

Poems by

Andrew Jones

Cover design by Shay Culligan

ISBN: 978-1-952326-53-0

Kelsay Books
502 South 1040 East, A-119
American Fork, Utah, 84003

For A & A

Acknowledgments

Many thanks to the editors of the journals where the following pieces first appeared:

Memoir Mixtapes: "Elegy for Jason Molina"
The Oakland Review: "Mixtape Composition"
Split Rock Review: "Skein" and "Ghost Ranch: Plein Air #1"
Foliate Oak: "College-town Estate Sale—Moorhead, MN"
Poetry Midwest: "Listening to Rain Fall and Thinking of Friends"
Barren Magazine: "Juntura"
Tattoo Highway: "Revelators"
Sierra Nevada Review: "Bourbon-bellied Cello"
North American Review: "Recipe for Reloading"

The poem "Bury Me with Hops" was originally printed under the title "Ode to Hops" as a limited-edition broadside for the opening of Dimensional Brewing Company in Dubuque, Iowa.

The poem "The Intro to Literature Professor's 115th Dream" was included in the anthology *Visiting Bob: Poems Inspired by the Life and Work of Bob Dylan* published by New Rivers Press, 2018.

Contents

I

I have enough treasures from the past
to last me longer than I need, or want.
—Anna Akhmatova, "March Elegy"

Liner Notes

[Windfall]

Steel guitar. Electric
crunch. Loping backbeat.
I pass hours browsing
through racks of used music

seeking this hybrid sound,
chancing purchases upon
eccentric band names
or cover art Americana.

Flip, flip, flip. Then
the clap of plastic
settling back:
zephyr of music.

[Live Free]

Eighteen-hundred miles
from the one home I've known,
the songs call like pick-up lines
from the Midwest.

I pen a break-up letter to California,
explain how the terrain lives
in the consonance of Minnesota.

Side-by-side with sinners
who fill the bars I haunt,
the music embraces me
from the intimacy of small stages.

[Tear Stained Eye]

In an old Civic,

she hauls me to the edges
of Dakota and Minnesota—

up the restless Red River to Grand Forks,
down back-road highways to Wahpeton,

across the Ojibwe words of Erdrich
and the revolutionary prairies of McGrath.

Every cassette mixtape I compose
to accompany broken-line sojourns:

a singular song.

[Route]

The meandering track
of the Mississippi
first comes to me
in song lyrics:
points of orientation
between
Itasca and New Orleans,
the sway of time
between
AM and FM.

I make devotions
and share vows
to the power of words.
She promises to keep
me in motion,
to teach me to love
sun dogs, the shake
of prairie grass,
and the surprise
of the Great Divide.

[Ten Second News]

Armed with words
such as petrichor, wild rice,
and lutefisk,
we boomerang
the land of sunsets
and flyover country.

First detour:
the soaked Northwest.

For nine months,
we honeymoon, flirt
with poetic lines
in used bookstores,
spend afternoons in bed,
and listen to the call
of vagabond bands.

Records//Conversations

You say: Pour the bourbon neat.
A finger at a time until I say stop.

Or, you say: Mix a brandy old-fashioned
weighted with extra cherries tonight.

I say: Pull the albums from the crates—
but only the ones you can't live without.

Share your burdens through song,
whispered lyrics or distorted guitars.

You say: Drop the needle in the groove,
call back some memory of your mother.

Or, you say: The gaps between the songs
aren't wide enough for my father's silence.

I say: The specks of lint & the liner note
dust are like the stars, the black vinyl opaque

as even the closest galaxy. And aren't we all
spinning around, hissing and popping.

My whole life's been a track that skips,
an old gatefold seam come unglued.

You say: Wait for the soft kiss of the needle.
How it hushes the room through the speakers,

before the treble rings in your teeth,
in your ligaments—look at your glass, *I say.*

The bass is lifting ripples over the surface
like a heartbeat, like a banded message.

You interrupt: Be still. Wait for the refrain.
There's so much for us to understand.

Elegy for Jason Molina

You might be holding the last light I see
—Songs: Ohia

You unfolded those old gas-station maps
in basement bars, carried me over highways,
& past lies waiting to trip me up. Songs lifted the moon
like a lantern & passed it over our secrets
giving shape to tenuous fibers of recognition.

You charted a course of fallen stars toward home.

You hinted at leaving: silence in the songs
like deep valleys vanquishing the North Star.
Yet departure, like the moment beyond a flash
of lightning, only deepened the darkness & rocked
the whippoorwills from their night branches.

Who would walk the midnight bridges with me now?

My guilt: wanting to keep you for myself.
I'd forgotten others navigate your catalogue
of verses. But this summer, between thunder & rain,
another voice lifted one of your melodies from a stage
in a prairie barn. I remembered to hold the ghosts I know,

and reckon with the ones who know I'll be coming.

Mixtape Composition

Understand the rhetorical situation:
this outweighs the academic and theoretical.
This is sit-at-the-bar-and-sweat-it-out
peer review. This is regret for never making
that phone call. So cut the world in half.
Arrangement is like an atlas: clear as Wyoming,
winding as Superior's silhouette, jagged
as city intersections. Avoid the suburbs—
so chronological.

Know your audience: is the desire for open space
restorative or a solitary introspection? Think
of backyard camaraderie, texts made of stars
and firepits. Be concerned with tempo, crescendo,
and reprieve. Remember that 808s too close to fiddle
cause vertigo. Remember a country funk tune
never harmed anyone. Leave pedal steel tracks
like possum prints across fresh snow…
everywhere and joyfully awkward.

Let the title do important work. Avoid puns,
the hits, the sing-alongs. This is about conveying
your stance—all pathos—your thesis implied.
Let your assembled voice lure like a stoned siren
singing on a summer night. Remember,
the softness of the final lyrical turn
should force a harder listen,
should demand
an echo.

Listening to Rain Fall and Thinking of Friends

after Thom Tammaro

Rain soaks the Pacific Northwest. Petrichor rises, reminds me
of friends. The wet streets leave no trace of others' steps as I tote
letters to the post office on gray afternoons. In Fargo, snow has
already fallen. I remember footprints burrowed in the spinster
snow of morning, and how the prints I kicked through, I might
have known.

Crows fly north come dusk, and I miss gaggles of Canadian geese
honking south at dawn. In this new western town, the nights still
rock with train cars screeching over tracks several blocks away.
Only now sugar beets are replaced by thundering loads of lumber,
whose sweet, damp scent nearly sickens me through open
windows.

I discover poems stashed in books, on postcards, in old email
folders—poems from friends sixteen hundred miles away. Reading
their words, the staunch drizzle on the roof fades. And I know
friends are using my name, keeping warm inside bars and houses
where sediment of my old life stashed and stored for moments
like these.

Ghost Ranch: Plein Air #1

At the core: pilsner meadow
slants left, rush of sage embraces

windsong, navigates & excoriates
Chimney Rock sandstone, steers

snow towards Cerro Pedernal in May.
The focus on distance here is too easy.

Don't let your eyes settle high upon bluff
and mesa, on exploding white clouds

cutting across the mirage of dusk sky:
purple thistle, starburst, the yellow

bloom show of yucca. Don't overlook
the meadow: low, earthy, muting & mixing

voices through the side-oats grama.
Always, the meadow crafts a swaying

hush, takes us as we come:
by heavy footfall or animal crawl.

Juntura

We've learned: the mind may turn to leaky vessel
with fealty and narrative tipping into emptiness.

So when we round the blind curve of Gold Creek
and the outline of the river birch makes no sense

against the backdrop of eastern Oregon, we call it
an omen, slow the car in the gravel and approach

its branches leafing out in shoes: sneakers, cleats,
boots, pointes—all with inked messages scrawled

on arches or insteps. We each remove a shoe,
print secrets for the other on the tongues. We knot

the dirtied laces to pair up the soles that have carried us
separately thus far, and offer them to high branches,

begging safe possession of our unsoiled hopes
before we ever have a chance to lose them.

Bury Me with Hops

When I die
bury me with hops
as companions.

O, Cascade! O, Mosaic!

may rhizomes
crown over me
each snowy spring.

O, Amarillo! O, Liberty!

run wild over
my torso, tighten
bines between my ribs.

O, Simcoe! O, Fuggles!

fill my bloodless heart
with lupulin—
sticky and neon gold.

O, Galaxy! O, Citra!

wolf of the soil,
bitter and preserve
my bones.

College-town Estate Sale—Moorhead, MN

We venture out on Saturday morning: snow falling, the thin
wipers of the old Civic paddling across the windshield, brushing
away heavy white clumps. The roads are unplowed and the
sidewalks need shoveling, but the forecast calls for inches more
during the day: no sense in clearing the path before it's likely to
be preserved. The car fishtails down 12th Avenue, through empty
intersections toward the western edge of Minnesota and the
address given to us by friends. They've proclaimed the exotic
and eerie treasures residing within the massive red house. Some
call it pastoral. Some, a hell of a bachelor pad. But the sale of the
old professor's bric-a-brac will be ending tomorrow: everything
must go.

The furrows of tires all seem to lead here, but there are only a few
cars parked in the dead end of the street. Unpruned for years, the
barren hedges rise up like grey moth-eaten waves capped with a
snowy froth. From the street, I can see only the top half of the
converted barn like a capsized boat in the distance. We stomp
clean our boots, remove gloves, and loosen our scarves on the
porch. The heat is turned low and by the front door the estate sale
crew hands out stale peppermint cookies and coffee. Women and
elderly couples shuffle through hallways into the spacious rooms,
paw antique china and unsorted bins of junk, fondle the polished
furniture. The price tags and markdowns draw out their smiles.
Not much has been gathered in the family room, and as we pass
through I'm pulled to the windows by the untouched, deep snow
slanting away in bright white down to the frozen river. So much
silence beyond the glass, and the falling snow only deepening the
layers of the history of cold.

We lose ourselves in two connecting rooms littered with books on
floor-to-ceiling metal racks. We could spend days sifting through
all of this but we haven't been given the hours to spare. You sat in
the man's lectures years ago, received papers marked with letters

in his hand. I've only heard his name over the last couple of days but feel awkward and intrusive handling his books—so many copies of Chaucer, Milton, Bronte, and Austen, as if owning every copy would lure in visitors and conversations. And in the books themselves, conversations in the margins and on title pages. There are dedications, notes of thanks, dates, inscriptions from and to people we float between: the names of the dead on campus buildings and once-young professors on the back cover who now mentor us and with whom we will drink warm orange liqueur this evening to stave off the cold of a plains winter. We part pages, participate in a silent conversation: part of the history of academia scattered about the city in used books.

There are more than books stashed on the shelves: magazines, yearbooks, cassettes, and theses. Some gems seem passed over just for us to find: a *New Yorker* from the week of my birth, a series of Russian translations, and literary LPs. On the lower shelves in the second room, the heavy vinyl rests in its sleeves under a fine layer of dust. We unearth old Caedmon record sets: readings by and of the works of Stein, Faulkner, Stevens, and Dylan Thomas. We choose our haul cautiously, weighing it on an imagined cosmic scale, leaving behind the books with penciled words too personal to remove—memories that don't feel quite right to breach.

I'm left with more questions than answers after the estate sale visit: the plentiful supply of women's dresses and garments in closets despite being an eternal bachelor; the copious amounts of a literary life heaped around the massive, ark-like house yet I'd never heard his name on campus; the use of narrow corridors to connect all the large rooms that blossomed into open spaces; the white, empty snow the only view from the windows.

We spend the last days of December huddled in our apartment near campus, wrapping up grades and commenting on papers. In the evenings, with the lights low, we listen to "A Child's Christmas in Wales"—one of the records we salvaged. More snow falls. It gets colder. And the old professor comes to life for me in these moments: his lectures in the brogue of Thomas, his movements like fluttering scraps of paper, his aura crafted of old books and dust. The white label of the record flurries around the turntable, spins out white like that long decline toward the Red River he stared at so many times alone.

II

It'll get so quiet when this record ends,
you can hear the first hour of the world...
 —Jason Molina, "The Big Game Is Every Night"

Liner Notes

[Drown]

I view Lock and Dam #11 on the Mississippi
from the bluff edges across the Driftless.

I never learned to swim,
but the water offers invitation—

a place to float until we catch a snag,
to hang on as long as possible.

River towns get waterlogged
or fill with the dead carcasses of fishflies—

so many lives hinging on humidity
and the slow lap of the water's edge.

[Loose String]

Before long, I pull her back to my coast.
Trying to tie up loose ends, we fray

the threads instead. Then we unravel a string
and a new life emerges. Every day in California

feels new: the gloom of June fog eases away,
opens up to brightness. Peel away a layer.

Roll up the sleeves. Start again. We listen close,
and try to learn lyrics we've misheard.

[Out of the Picture]

Rivers have never been alone
in churning and moving. Trends
and downturns push us back
over roads I never expect
to travel again. Nobody flees
California. Who returns to Iowa?

What was once in the rearview
and received a goodbye note,
suddenly rises inside
the horizon of the windshield—
a different Honda deciphering
the Morse code of interstate lines.

[Catching On]

I become accustomed
to tornado sirens, forget
the feel of earthquakes
and the shimmer of gold hills.

Seasons turn in fourths now
and the sun falls so far away.

A method for adjustment:
drop roots in the driftless soil
and learn to pronounce words
the midwestern way.

[Too Early]

I think my father's death
will unspool music
like split 8-track tape.

In the void he leaves,
I find a buried playlist

planted half my lifetime ago:
obscure players and chords
waiting to cycle around

and fill the silence
like a dirge of cicadas.

[Mystifies Me]

The lyrics catch me—so serendipitous
they make a nonbeliever want to believe.

I hear the songs, alone
in my bedroom,

hear the songs
rotating highway miles,

and hear the songs
held in her arms.

Now, I sing out
and a daughter harmonizes.

Repeat to me the memories
linked to sound: images

played over notes,
meandering like the Mississippi;

life as a song.

Last Visit to Joshua Tree

Seeking ghosts & direction
I plot the path to Cap Rock:
the Grievous Angel's mythic pyre.

Camp built, sunset
resurrects landscape—
tree branches explode
like fuzzy stars, shift
like ragged nightmares.

Against fever dream horizon
this valley is: the moon's surface. Or:
the edge of a wildfire approaching.

Across uneven ground
the arboreal dead rise—
bark-and-shadow bastards—
uproot & drag me
to new compass points.

Revelators

for Gillian Welch & David Rawlings

In a black house dress, hunched over that full-bodied
blonde guitar, her strumming is persistent, her rusty hair
sways over pale skin, and she keeps time with her right foot—
cowboy boot twisting out mythical ashes.
Her high-lonesome whisper calls to me a gospel
ready-made for my ancestors buried in Wisconsin soil,
ready-made to direct me to grace.

His nasal vocals fall not behind or in front, but receive hers.
A grey-suited marionette shaking loose the strings
on his parlor-sized archtop, his toes staked to the wooden stage
while his body rolls with electricity. With his eyes closed
under thick brown bangs, his long delicate fingers
wrench and press the bronze strings so far
down the neck it is nearly a sin.

Sing to me again, that line of Lazarus waiting
behind the window shade to reveal his scars.
Pull me through that hymn book so worn,
so thick with devotion, filled by allegory and melody.
And I'll sing, I'll testify to this haunted pair
on the bare stage in a white, domed marble hall
as still as a mausoleum.

Sonnenizio on a Line from Disch

Although I'm past the halfway point, I still
read over my life in boxes, note points
of departure and pointless labels like valuables
or knick-knacks. The point is: I've hauled cardboard
across twelve states, layered tape to the point
it serves as a disappointing symbol
for the waypoint where one epoch
pointed to a new zip code. I can trace
the dead insects like needlepoint patterns
appointed on the cardboard roadmap.
Every endpoint has never been the end:
just a dewpoint, a weathervane; just
coordinates for a future starting point;
everything arranged in counterpoint.

Bourbon-bellied Cello

for Ben Sollee

Let the rosined bow
slide across the taut strings—
a quartet of rich veins.
Let it cut deep.
Let the music spill
from the bourbon-bellied cello
into and across the old floorboards
of our small bungalow.
So percussive are the tones,
so deep are the vibrations
that our daughter is swept up
in the ebb and flow.
She begins a toddler's waltz:
awkwardly stepping and twirling,
her hair floating in the air
a half-movement behind.
As her tiny feet tap out
a jagged staccato
our calamitous house
distills to a sliver of bliss.

The Intro to Literature Professor's 115th Dream

8AM: A musty Catholic college classroom.
"Where Are You Going, Where Have You Been?"
I offer to the silence, "Let's start with the dedication,"
queue up "It's All Over Now, Baby Blue," press play,
and close my eyes: Dylan slants behind the lectern—
some Flannery O'Connor misfit or Arnold Friend

in the flesh, sneering and foreboding like the pied piper
of the footnotes, a vagabond who doesn't need a gun,
just surly asides, just hijacked syntax
that rocks and shakes these kids awake,
that tells them where it's at, where they're going,
and prepares them for the second coming of Bob.

Skein

As a kid, the Canadas always fascinated me.
So few descended in the Sacramento Valley
among the tule fog and rice fields. The deeper
pitch, the driftwood underbelly, and banded
black neck such a welcome contrast
against the impervious Snows.

"Honkers," my dad would say, pointing at some speck
on the horizon, impressing me with his vision
and knowledge, "Branta canadensis." The birds
appeared to me only upon his encouraging. Our backs
pressed into the rice checks, we watched their lilting flight
carry on through the dampness toward the Black Buttes.

Only in those fields of Richmond Hunting Club
was my father infallible and at peace. I learned
to appreciate the strained echo of the Snow geese
rising in swirling swift masses, like storms
I would later fear rolling across the plains
toward my new home in the old Dacotah Territory.

A quarter-century gone, I stand at the edge of Iowa,
search for the skein of honkers I hear approaching
from some vast place I still fail to see. They break
the cloud bottoms, the silent edge of gloom,
shadows dropping in blowing snow. In the numb cold,
I wait for his voice and listen to their beating wings.

Odortype

While your father worked swing shift,
you plunged a face in his pillow
and breathed deep his smell.
Thirty years on, it comes back—
sweat, toasted malt, and Marlboro reds—
after mistaking a stranger for the dead.

Your mother's aroma is a recipe—
wildflowers, sun, sugar, and cinnamon—
baked thirty minutes at 350 degrees.
It unfurls from care packages
sent cross-country to your daughter.
How can such a fragile thing travel so far?

Will your daughter recall the bitterness
of hops in trying to describe your scent?
Or the warm comfort of sourdough?
Might she name the fragrance you wear
as silence? It's the odor you can't find
a chemical strong enough to wash away.

Recipe for Reloading

Canisters of smokeless powder. Canvas sacks of lead shot. Yellow wads in clear plastic bags. Boxes of paper shotshells. Brass primers. These were the ingredients of your father's cookbook.

He spent hours in the single-car garage with his endless supply of Marlboro reds filling the rafters with smoke. He bellied up to the workbench on a barstool, the cracks in the vinyl seat mended with the metallic gray of duct tape. His laboratory spread before him on the workbench: tumbler, scale, funnel, reloading press with its cylinders marked by measurement lines, and small trays to catch spent primers. A silver Sears 8-track stereo receiver, tuned to KFOG in San Francisco, sat at the far end of the formica-topped workbench.

You were always welcome in the garage while your father worked reloading shotshells for hunting trips. He let you hold the funnel while he poured shot or pull the lever to crimp the ends of the shells. Sometimes he poured a bit of powder in a steel tray, set it outside the screen door of the garage, and lowered his cigarette into it, setting off a fuzzy flame like the fireworks that were illegal in California. He always talked to you about the music coming from the radio and sometimes thrilled you by calling in a request to the station—almost always "Treetop Flyer" by Stephen Stills or something by Robin Trower.

Your father searched for the perfect reloading recipes in small, spiral-bound books. He considered the primer burn rates, the grains and blends of powder, the length of the wad. He talked velocity in feet per second, imagining how much time one might be able to gain on a high-flying pintail or a pheasant weaving through a tangle of fallen trees along a creek edge.

Before you ever fired a shotgun on your own, you could reload a shotshell without a mistake. You knew how to set the primer, fill the powder, place the wad, slide the lever to switch cylinders and let the shot funnel into the shell. And you carried these shells in the pockets of your oversized camouflage rain gear through the damp, mucky mornings in the Sacramento valley, gladly handing over your finished products for your father to slide into the chamber of the Remington you would one day shoulder in the same rice fields and ditches.

It has been decades since you worked the reloading press but many times since your father's death you've dreamed of reloading one recipe. In the dream, the screen door to the backyard is open and through it the fog comes in across the Bay at the edge of sunset. You push the lime-green 8-track tape of Robin Trower's 1974 album, *Bridge of Sighs*, into the stereo—the album your father played constantly in his GMC pickup on the drive north up I-5— and "In this Place" plays loud and deep.

Your father has written out the details of the recipe on a yellowed sheet in a small, spiral-bound notebook—measurements of all the basics, plus his own name between steps for inserting the wad and dropping the shot. You move through the process swiftly, sure of yourself and trusting the recipe. Sitting among the ingredients is the simple urn that houses your father's ashes and has rested in the same place in your mother's family room for five years. You don't hesitate as you funnel what remains of him into the paper shotshell before pulling the lever to crimp the end shut.

You step out the screen door into what has become a burnt rice field at sunrise. The Remington .20 gauge your grandfather bought upon returning from World War II rests in the crook of your arm and you slide in one of the shells filled with ashes. Up ahead, the old black lab of your childhood flushes a rooster pheasant from the safety of blackberry bushes at the edge of a ditch. You can feel the pressure of the trigger pushing back as you squeeze it, sending your father so many feet per second into the future before you.

You always wake without knowing if the pheasant flutters and falls or flies on beating its wings furiously. You always wake knowing you're not yet brave enough to follow the recipe you're certain you can find in one of the small, spiral-bound books your father left waiting for you on his workbench.

Notes

"Windfall," "Live Free," "Tear Stained Eye," "Route," "Ten Second News," "Drown," "Loose String," "Out of the Picture," "Catching On," "Too Early," and "Mystifies Me": These are the eleven songs on Son Volt's debut album, *Trace*. The album was released by Warner Bros. records on September 19th, 1995 and has served as a steady companion and soundtrack for my life in five states over the last two decades. These songs served as inspiration for crafting a "liner note" poem that used each song title as part of a longer sequence. Read together, they make up one long poem with eleven sections. Read dispersed, they serve as notes or guides to the other poems in the collection.

"Elegy for Jason Molina": The epigraph is a Molina lyric from "Hold On Magnolia" off of *The Magnolia Electric Co.* by Songs: Ohia.

"Ghost Ranch: Plein Air #1": Ghost Ranch is an education and retreat center in Abiquiu, New Mexico. It was the home of Georgia O'Keeffe.

"Juntura": The shoe tree is located on US Hwy 20 about 17 miles east of Juntura, Oregon. The original shoe tree was burned down but a nearby tree has since been turned into a shoe tree.

"Last Visit to Joshua Tree": The Grievous Angel is a reference to musician Gram Parsons. After his death, his body was stolen by friends and taken to Joshua Tree National Park, where they attempted to burn his remains near Cap Rock.

"Sonnenizio on a Line from Disch": The sonnenizio form was invented by Kim Addonizio. It requires using a line from another sonnet and then choosing one word from the line to repeat in the following thirteen lines of the poem. The first line of this poem is taken from "A Bookmark" by Tom Disch from *Yes, Let's!: New and Selected Poems,* Johns Hopkins University Press, 1989.

"The Intro to Literature Professor's 115th Dream": Arnold Friend is a character in Joyce Carol Oates's short story, "Where Are You Going, Where Have You Been?" which was dedicated to Bob Dylan. The mention of a misfit is an allusion to Flannery O'Connor's story, "A Good Man Is Hard to Find."

"Mystifies Me": Though this song is on Son Volt's album, *Trace,* it was originally written and recorded by Ron Wood. It appears on the album, *I've Got My Own Album to Do,* released by Warner Records.

About the Author

Andrew Jones is Assistant Professor of English and Creative Writing at the University of Dubuque, where he coordinates the Archway Reading & Lecture Series. His previous works include *Moving Like Dim Ghosts* (2016) and the collaborative chapbook *Songenizios* (2020). He serves as an Assistant Editor and Book Reviewer for *Split Rock Review*.

Made in the USA
Middletown, DE
12 October 2020

21755099R00031